BATH SPA UNIVERSITY
DISCARD
NEWTON PARK
LIBRARY

D1188913

Reading eggs

My First
High Frequency Words

By Sara Leman

Ages 5–7

B.S.U.C. - LIBRARY

00340115

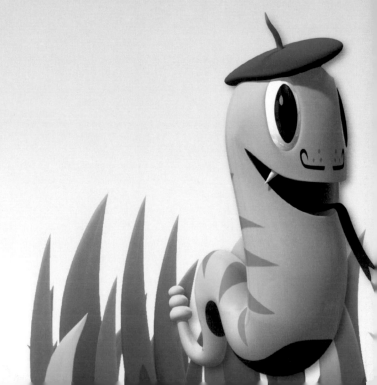

This book is part of the **My First** series of **Reading Eggs** workbooks. **Reading Eggs** has proven to be very popular with parents, children and teachers. The **Reading Eggs** books and website have helped more than 200,000 children learn to read.

Each vibrant book in the **My First** series includes a wide range of interesting activities that will help your child develop essential reading and writing skills. Written by experienced teachers and educators, the series supports what your child learns at school.

The pages are clear and uncluttered, with activities that build real skills. Activities are fun and motivate children to continue working and learning. Instructions are easy to follow and regular challenges entice children to extend their learning.

We hope that you and your child enjoy using this and other books in the series.

Reading eggs

Published by Wayland in 2015
Copyright © Blake Publishing 2011
All rights reserved.
ISBN: 978-0-7502-9497-3
10 9 8 7 6 5 4 3 2 1

MIX
Paper from responsible sources
FSC® C104740
FSC
www.fsc.org

Wayland, an imprint of Hachette Children's Group
Part of Hodder & Stoughton
Carmelite House, 50 Victoria Embankment, London EC4Y 0DZ

Written by Sara Leman
Publisher: Katy Pike
Editors: Sandra Iannella and Amanda Santamaria
Design and layout by Modern Art Production Group

An Hachette UK Company
www.hachette.co.uk
www.hachettechildrens.co.uk

Contents

Suggestions for activities to do at home

- Old magazines and junk mail can be used for a variety of activities including:
  - searching for and circling particular words, such as **only, these, now**
  - cutting out individual letters or sight words to create a collage e.g. **words that begin with 'o'**.

- Allow your child to play with magnetic letters on the fridge to create words. Rearrange the letters to make new words, e.g. **when = we, he, new, hen**.

Create crosswords, e.g.

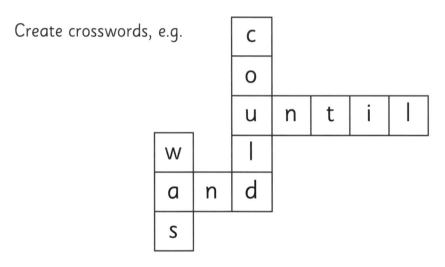

- Encourage your child to write high frequency words on steamed-up mirrors and windows at home and in the car.

- Trace words on your child's back and ask them to guess what you have written. Alternatively, ask your child to trace words in the air with their finger.

- Allow your child to create words in shaving foam, sand, paint, playdough, string or pavement chalk.

- Play a variation of 'hangman'. Choose a word that the child knows and ask them to fill in the blanks. Alternatively, play 'What am I writing?' Write the first letter of the word and ask your child to guess what the word might be. Then write the second letter and so on until your child guesses correctly or the word is complete.

- Making simple flashcards for your child is a great way to reinforce high frequency words. Activities to try include:
  - Give me a sentence. Choose 5 sight words and write each word on a card. Ask your child to choose a card and to give you a sentence that uses that high frequency word. Repeat with the remaining cards.
  - Listen to the sentence. Say a sentence aloud to your child and emphasise the high frequency within it. Ask your child to try to locate the high frequency word from a small selection of flashcards. This activity will help your child to make the association between the spoken and written word.
  - Unscrambling sentences. Make up a simple sentence e.g. **How are you today?** Write each word on a flashcard and shuffle the cards. Lay them out and let your child unscramble the sentence. Point out clues such as a capital letter at the start of the sentence and the punctuation mark at the end.
  - Bingo. Create a 3 × 2 grid for your child and fill it with 6 high frequency words.
  Write matching words on flashcards. Select a flashcard, read the word aloud to your child and encourage them to cross off the corresponding word on their grid.
  - Concentration. Choose 6 high frequency words and write each word on two cards. Shuffle the cards and lay them face down. The child turns over one card at a time and has to try to remember where the matching word is in order to make a pair.
  - Snap. This can be played using the flashcards from the 'concentration' activity. 'Snap' and 'concentration' games help to build your child's visual recognition skills.

- Laminate a plain piece of A4 paper. Use a marker and write one of the tricky high frequency words, for example **because**. Use the laminated paper as a table placemat for your child. Encourage your child to look at the word and say the word aloud a few times before each meal. Once the word has been committed to memory, wipe it off and write a new one.

Word chart

List of 96 words covered

so	her	go
we	with	me
the	here	he
to	then	do
as	than	has
and	they	can
but	some	put
how	give	now
see	little	saw
for	which	of
his	could	him
you	said	your
are	about	from
one	all	on
in	because	into
my	also	why

after	no	other
this	be	that
there	she	where
when	too	what
these	was	thing
them	any	their
come	got	done
have	were	leave
better	say	pretty
who	not	while
would	it	should
again	our	pair
out	more	house
shall	only	will
before	until	been
always	by	along

1 Trace and copy each word.

so   no   go

_____   _____   _____

2 Colour so = red, colour no = blue, colour go = green.

no   go

so   no

go   so

so   no

3 Complete.

S_____   ____o____   g_____

8

4 **Guess the word by its shape. Write each word in a box.**

so   no   go

5 **Circle the correct word. Cross out the wrong word.**

A green light tells you to go   no .

Happy Nap is go   so sleepy.

There are no   so chips for Charlie Chimp.

You can no   go with Sam the Ant.

We were running so   go late.

CHALLENGE Circle the hidden words.

algortsomnovtgovwsorno

9

Lesson 2 • we, me, be

1 **Join each letter to Me Be Fish. Write the words.**

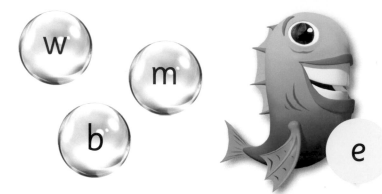

_____

_____

_____

2 **Colour we = red, colour me = blue, colour be = yellow.**

be we me

me we be

we be me

3 **Write the words in alphabetical order.**

we be me

_____ _____ _____

4 Read the clue. Write the word.

A word that means

myself. _____

A word that means

us. _____

5 Complete the sentences.

me　We　be

_____ can see Issy Me on a flower.

Tom the Dog will _____ here soon.

Meg the Hen gave _____ an egg.

CHALLENGE

Write the word me.
Draw a picture of
yourself. Write
these labels:

head body
arms legs

11

1 Trace and write the words.

he   the   she

_____   _____   _____

2 Match the word to its picture.

he

she

3 Colour the word the.

the

the

he

me

be

the

the

the

4 **Help Sid the Kid get to the park.**
Draw a track of he the she words.

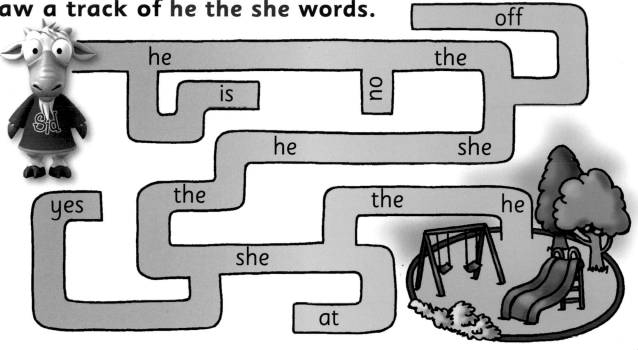

5 **Circle the words.**

He She the

Jazz the Cat has a hat. She loves her hat. Sam the Ant has a bag. He wants a new bag.

Colour a star each time you find a word.

CHALLENGE
Write sentences using these words.
he   the   she

13

Lesson 4 • to, do, too

1 Help Smile do his washing. Colour the path of to words.

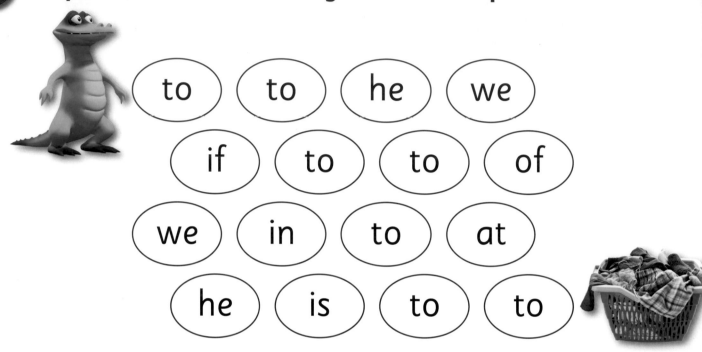

to	to	he	we
if	to	to	of
we	in	to	at
he	is	to	to

2 Trace and write the words.

to   do   too

_____   _____   _____

Complete the words.

 t    d    oo

14

3 Crack the code!

o = ✿
t = ★
d = ■
n = ✓

1 ★ ✿ ✿

_____

2 ■ ✿

_____

3 ★ ✿

_____

4 ✓ ✿

_____

5 ✿ ✓

_____

6 ✓ ✿ ★

_____

4 Complete the sentences.

to   Do   too

_____ you like Gemma's big bow?

Can I have some cake _____ ?

Give the bone _____ Tom the Dog.

 **CHALLENGE** Write or draw a list of:

"Things I can do".

1 Colour as = blue, colour has = green, colour was = red.

was   as   has   was

has   as

2 Join the letters. Write the words.

has   was   as

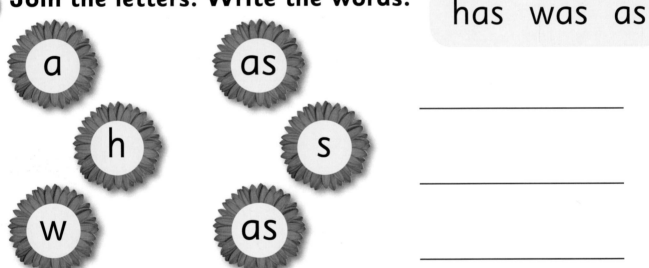

a   as

h   s

w   as

_____

_____

_____

3 Guess the word by its shape. Write each word in a box.

as   has   was

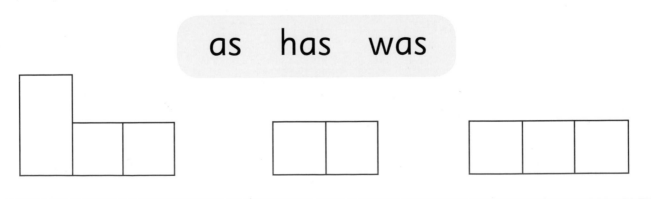

4 **Write the words in alphabetical order.**

 was    as    has

_____   _____   _____

5 **Circle the correct word. Cross out the wrong word.**

It   was   has   Dan's birthday.

Yetiyo   has   as   lots of yoyos.

I can jump   was   as   far as Kangako.

CHALLENGE

Look for the words

as   has   was

in an old magazine or newspaper. Cut them out and glue them on paper. Write a sentence for each word.

17

Lesson 6 • and, can, any

1 Join Sandy Can to the word **can**.

can

yes

can

can

no

can

on

2 Write **and** in the middle of each pair.

burger _____ fries

knife _____ fork

shoes _____ socks

bucket _____ spade

3

SHELLY'S SHOP

Colour yes or no.

Does she have any cups? (yes) (no)

Does she have any bags? (yes) (no)

Does she have any dogs? (yes) (no)

Does she have any hats? (yes) (no)

4 **Join the words that rhyme.**

and   man

can   Penny

any   hand

CHALLENGE Write down 5 things that you can do.

I can _____ .

1 Trace and copy each word.

_____   _____   _____

2 Colour **but** = blue, colour **put** = pink, colour **got** = green.

but

put

put

got

got

but

put

got

3 Complete.

b _ t   _ut   g___

4 **Guess the word by its shape. Write each word in a box.**

but   put   got

5 **Circle the correct word. Cross out the wrong word.**

Put   But   your rubbish in the bin.

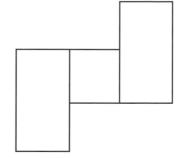

I have   put   got   a puppy.

Shoe Sheep wears shoes
but   put   not socks.

CHALLENGE Circle the hidden words.

abutggotflputbbutngotvput

21

1 **Find the matching words.**

how	now	were
now	were	how
were	how	now

2 **Help Tick Tock Clock find his watch. Colour the path of now words.**

now   now   go   low

so   now   now   row

how   on   now   to

cow   bow   now   now

3 **Complete the words.**

h u _____   _____ ow   _____ ere

4 **Answer the questions.**

How many?

How big?

 3 m

How old?

____

____

____

5 **Circle the words.**

How Now Were

How are you Icy Mice? Were you playing in the snow? Now you can make a snowman. How big can you make it?

Colour a snowball each time you find a word.

◯ ◯ ◯ ◯

CHALLENGE

Find a rhyming word from your list for:

cow wow her

1 Join each word to a picture that rhymes.

go

me

too

and

can

got

how

no

2 Write the words in the correct box.

we   any
the   do
to   put

2 letter words

3 letter words

③ Find the words. Colour:

so = pink   were = red
be = blue   but = green
was = yellow   he = orange

s	o	w	a	s	w	e	r	e	h	e
b	u	t	w	e	r	e	b	e	s	o
h	e	w	e	r	e	b	e	w	a	s
s	o	b	e	b	u	t	w	e	r	e
w	a	s	h	e	w	e	r	e	s	o
b	e	w	e	r	e	s	o	b	u	t
w	a	s	w	e	r	e	s	o	b	e
h	e	b	e	w	e	r	e	b	u	t
w	a	s	s	o	h	e	w	e	r	e
w	e	r	e	b	u	t	h	e	b	e
w	a	s	h	e	w	e	r	e	s	o
b	e	w	e	r	e	b	u	t	h	e

1 Colour see = green, colour saw = red, colour say = yellow.

see say

saw see

say see

saw say

2 Join the letters. Write the words.

see saw say

s

aw

s

ay

s

ee

_____

_____

_____

3 Join the words to a picture.

see

say

4 Crack the code!

s = ❀
e = ★
a = ✓
y = ■
w = ●

1 ❀ ★ ★ _____

2 ❀ ✓ ■ _____

3 ❀ ✓ ● _____

4 ● ✓ ❀ _____

5 ✓ ❀ _____

6 ■ ★ ❀ _____

5 Complete the sentences.

Say   see   saw

Did you _____ Flobby today?

I _____ Me Be Fish yesterday.

_____ hello to Sid the Kid.

CHALLENGE Write 5 things down that you can see.

27

1 Trace and copy each word.

  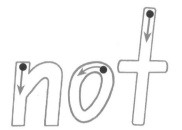

_____ _____ _____

2 Colour the word for.

for

car

for

of

for

for

or

for

from

3 Unjumble the words. Write them.

f o   o t n   r f o

_____   _____   _____

4 **Complete.** not

You can _____ swim.

You can _____ ride.

You can _____ skate.

5 **Circle the correct word. Cross out the wrong word.**

I love to eat lots for   of cake.

Jake has a gift not   for you.

Grumble Goz is of   not happy.

I am ready for   of bed.

CHALLENGE
Write sentences using these words.

of   not   for

Lesson 11 • his, him, it

1 Join Dan to the word him.

him

him

her

he

him

him

him

2 Complete the labels.

his

his head

_____ eye

_____ ear

_____ tusk

_____ trunk

_____ leg

3 Join the words to the pictures.

it

him

4 Guess the word by its shape. Write each word in a box.

his   him   it

5 Join the words that rhyme.

his   swim

him   lit

it   fizz

CHALLENGE Circle the hidden words.

whiszhimvitnhisohimmit

1 Find the matching words.

you   our   your

your   you   our

our   your   you

2 Help Ayee I Owe You to get his money. Colour the path of you words.

you   you   out   yes

our   you   you   your

over   you   you   yell

your   our   you   you

3 Complete the words.

_y_____   _____our   _____ur

32

4 Read the clue. Write the word.

Belonging to you. _____

Belonging to us. _____

5 Complete the sentences.

your   our   you

Can _____ see Rocky Robot?

Is this _____ sock, Socky Fox?

Fluff the Duck swims in _____ pond.

Can _____ give me
a ride, Tug Boat Bug?

CHALLENGE Look for the words
you   your   our
in an old magazine or newspaper.
Cut them out and glue them on paper.
Write a sentence for each word.

1 Colour **are** = red, colour **more** = blue, colour **from** = green.

| are | more | from | are | more |

| from | are | more | from | are |

2 Trace and copy each word.

_____   _____   _____

3 Circle the matching words in each row.

are	our	are	ate
more	move	mare	more
from	form	from	farm

3 Help Bee Bee Bear to get more honey. Draw a track of are more from words.

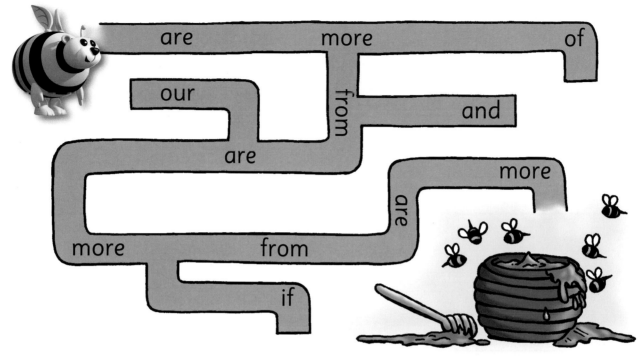

are   more   of

our

from

and

are

more

are

more

from

if

4 Circle the words.

Are   more   from

Are you there, Smile? I have a letter from Meg the Hen. She has got more eggs for you.

Colour a letter each time you find a word.

CHALLENGE
Write a letter to Smile the Crocodile from Meg the Hen.

1 Draw.

Only one eye on
Slip and Slide.

Blue Wing sitting
on her nest.

2 Guess the word by its shape. Write each word in a box.

one   only   on

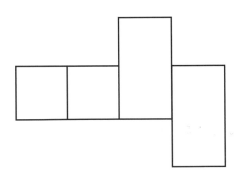

3 Complete the words.

_____ n   on _____   on _____

4 Crack the code!

o = ▲
n = ●
e = ★
l = ■
y = ✓
s = ❀

1 ▲ ● _____

2 ▲ ● ★ _____

3 ▲ ● ■ ✓ _____

4 ● ▲ _____

5 ✓ ★ ❀ _____

6 ❀ ▲ _____

5 Circle the words.

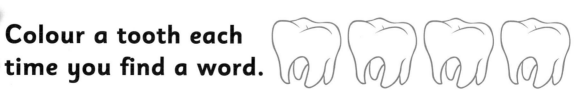

one   only   on

Zeewee plays on the swings. He is funny!

He has only got one tooth and one eye.

Colour a tooth each time you find a word.

★ **CHALLENGE**
Write sentences using the words.

one   only   on

1 **Join Insillysect to the word into.**

into

to

on

into

into

in

into

2 **Trace and copy each word.**

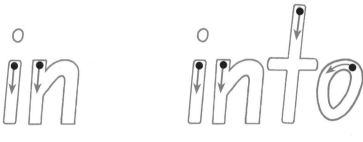

_____   _____   _____

3 **Circle the word into.**

Pram Lamb got into her pram.

Fluff the Duck got into her bath.

4 **Colour yes or no.**

Where is Big Pig?

Is he **in** the sea? yes no

Is he **in** the park? yes no

Is he **in** bed? yes no

Is he **in** some mud? yes no

5 **Circle the correct word. Cross out the wrong word.**

You can not eat the cake into   until it is ready.

Jump until   into the bath!

Wait there in   until it is time to go.

Lots of fish swim in   until the sea.

CHALLENGE **Circle the hidden words.**
cinvintogluntilwrinfinto

1 Trace and copy each word.

my   why   by

_____   _____   _____

2 Find the matching words.

(my)   (why)   (by)

(why)   (by)   (my)

(by)   (my)   (why)

3 Complete.

m_____   wh_____   _____y

4 **Label Nutty Newt's things.**

my

This is _____ scarf.

This is _____ hat.

This is _____ sock.

This is _____ bag.

This is _____ shoe.

5 **Complete the sentences.**

my   Why   by

_____ are you sad, Alphapet?

Gemma Giraffe has got _____ hat.

Frogfish sits _____ the river.

Ding Bat sleeps in _____ tree.

CHALLENGE
Write 4 questions that start with Why.
Remember to put a ? at the end.

41

1 Join the matching words.

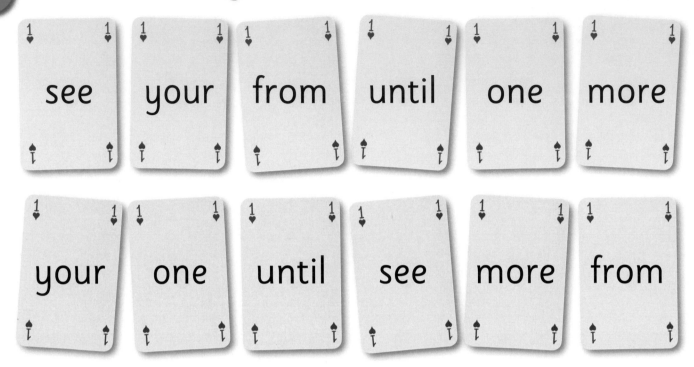

see   your   from   until   one   more

your   one   until   see   more   from

2 Colour 2-letter words = red, 3-letter words = yellow and 4-letter words = green.

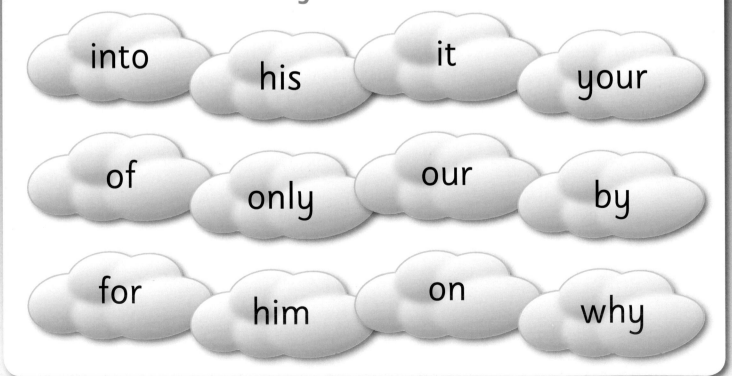

into   his   it   your

of   only   our   by

for   him   on   why

3 **Power words. Join the words that rhyme.**

see

my

got

how

to

but

go

your

more

rut

now

do

by

me

not

no

1 Help Airy Fairy find her wand. Colour the path of her words.

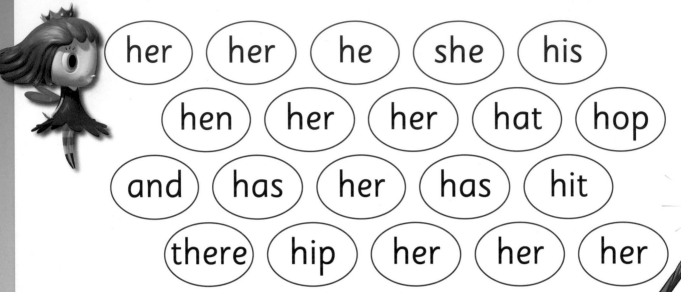

2 Colour the answers.

What comes **after**  ?

What comes **after**  ?

What comes **after**  ?

3 Guess the word by its shape. Write each word in a box.

her after other

4 Write each word in alphabetical order.

other   after   her

_____   _____   _____

5 Circle the correct word. Cross out the wrong word.

Shoe Sheep loves after   her new shoes.

Socky Fox likes his her   other socks best of all.

Tom the Dog will play after other he has had a bone.

CHALLENGE
How many words can you make from the letters
o t h e r. (You can only use each letter once.)
2 good! 3 great!! +4 WOW!!!

45

1 Colour **with** = blue, colour **this** = red, colour **that** = green.

with   this   that   with

that   with   this   that

2 Circle the matching words in each row.

with	what	when	with
this	those	this	the
that	than	thin	that

3 Trace and copy each word.

with   this   that

_____   _____   _____

4 **Make words with these letters.**

2-letter word:

3-letter word:

4-letter word:

5 **Circle the words.**

with   This   that

This is Lollipop Mop, and that is Thistle. They are going to the shops with Shelley. This is going to be fun!

Colour a star each time you find a word.

CHALLENGE Look for the words
with   this   that
in an old magazine or newspaper.
Cut them out and glue them on paper.
Write a sentence for each word.

47

1 **Join the word to a picture that rhymes.**

where   here   there

2 **Colour there = red, colour where = blue, colour here = green.**

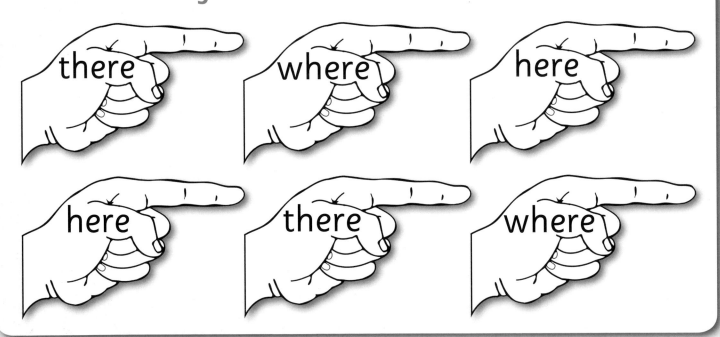

there   where   here

here   there   where

3 **Complete the words.**

h_____   th_____   wh_____

4 Help Flutter Bye Bye fly from here to there. Draw a track of here there where words.

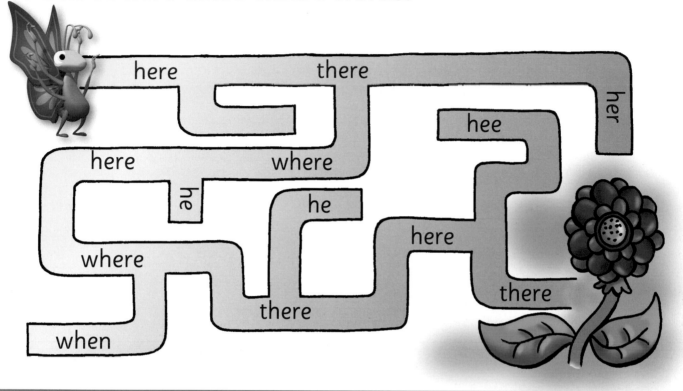

here   there   her

hee

here   where

he   he

here

where

there

there

when

5 Complete the sentences.

Here   there   Where

_____ are you, Octo Puss?

_____ you are!

Let's play over _____.

CHALLENGE

Write 4 questions that start with Where.
Remember to put a ? at the end.

49

Lesson 20 • then, when, what

1 Circle the word hen in these words:

then   when

Circle the word hat in this word:

what

2 Colour when = red, colour what = green.

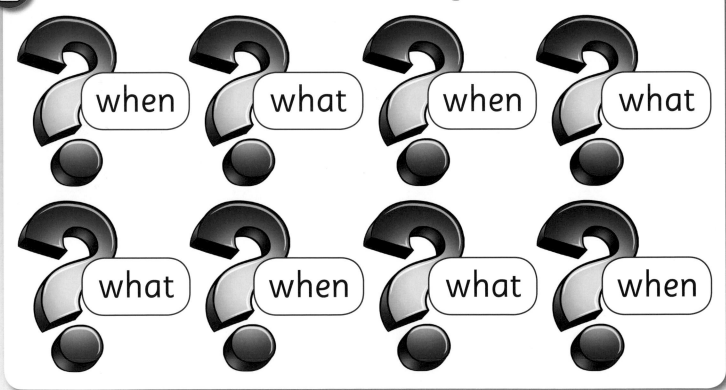

when   what   when   what

what   when   what   when

3 Complete the words.

t_____   ___hen   w_____

50

4 **Crack the code!**

t = ❀
h = ★
e = ■
n = ●
w = ✓
a = ▲

1 ✓ ★ ■ ●

_____

2 ✓ ★ ▲ ❀

_____

3 ❀ ★ ■ ●

_____

4 ❀ ★ ■

_____

5 ★ ■

_____

6 ✓ ■ ● ❀

_____

5 **Circle the correct word. Cross out the wrong word.**

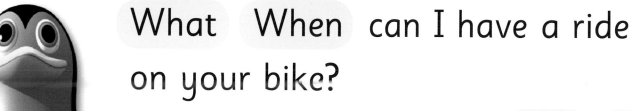

When   What are you doing, Pinkipoo?

What   When can I have a ride on your bike?

First we will have cake, then   what we will have ice cream. Yum!

CHALLENGE
Write 4 questions that start with What or When. Remember to put a ? at the end.

51

1 **Join Thingamabob to the word thing.**

thing

that

then

thing

thing

thing

this

2 **Complete the sentences.** than

Underting

Octo Puss

Eggyphant

Octo Puss is bigger _____ Underting.

Eggyphant is bigger _____ Octo Puss.

Underting is smaller _____ Eggyphant.

3 **Make words with these letters.**

e t e s h

2-letter word: ◯ ◯

3-letter word: ◯ ◯ ◯

5-letter word: ◯ ◯ ◯ ◯ ◯

4 **Complete the sentences.**

than   these   thing

Are _____ your socks, Socky Fox?

Are you bigger _____ Jazz the Cat?

This _____ belongs to

Go Go Gizmo and _____

carrots must be Red Rabbit's.

CHALLENGE
Write sentences using these words.

than   these   thing

Lesson 22 • they, them, their

1 Join the word to a picture that rhymes.

they

them

their

2 Trace and copy each word.

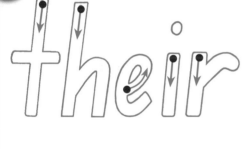

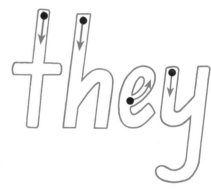

_____

_____

_____

3 Join the letters. Write the words.

th ey

th em

th eir

_____

_____

_____

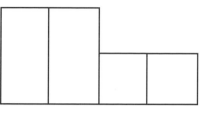

4 Guess the word by its shape. Write each word in a box.

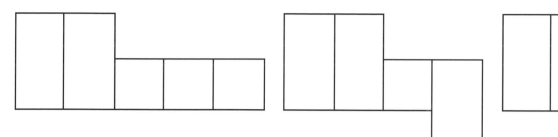
they   them   their

5 Label their things.   their

 gloves

_____ socks

_____ boots

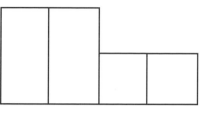
_____ hats

_____ scarves

6 Circle the words.   They   them   their

This is Tom and Dogfin. I play with them at their house. They are funny.

Colour a bone each time you find a word.

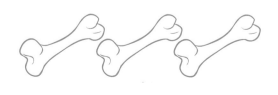

1 Colour some = green, come = red, done = blue.

some come done come some done

2 Circle the matching words in each row.

some	so	same	some
come	came	cone	come
done	don't	done	does

3 Guess the word by its shape. Write each word in a box.

4 Help Shoe Sheep to find some shoes. Draw a track of some come done words.

some came same

done done

say some

come some can't

don't can

5 Complete the sentences.

done some come

Bee Bee Bear has _____ honey for me.

Can Baby Face _____ to my party?

Have you _____ all of your jobs, Lollipop Mop?

CHALLENGE
Write down 3 things that you have done today.
I have done...

1 Join the pieces. Write the words.

_____

_____

_____

2 Colour yes or no.

I **have** one eye.   yes no

I **have** ten legs.   yes no

I **have** one tooth.   yes no

I **have** blue hair.   yes no

3 Complete the words.

giv _____   ___*ave*   *lea*__*e*

4 Follow the instructions.

Give Marshmallow Mouse a big, pink hat.

Give Smile the Crocodile an apple pie.

5 Circle the correct word. Cross out the wrong word.

Please have give me that ball.

What time does your train leave give ?

I leave have not washed my hands.

CHALLENGE
Write these words in alphabetical order.

leave give have

Choose one word to write in a sentence.

1 **Colour: her = red, with = green, here = yellow, then = pink, they = orange, some = blue, give = purple, after = brown, this = black**

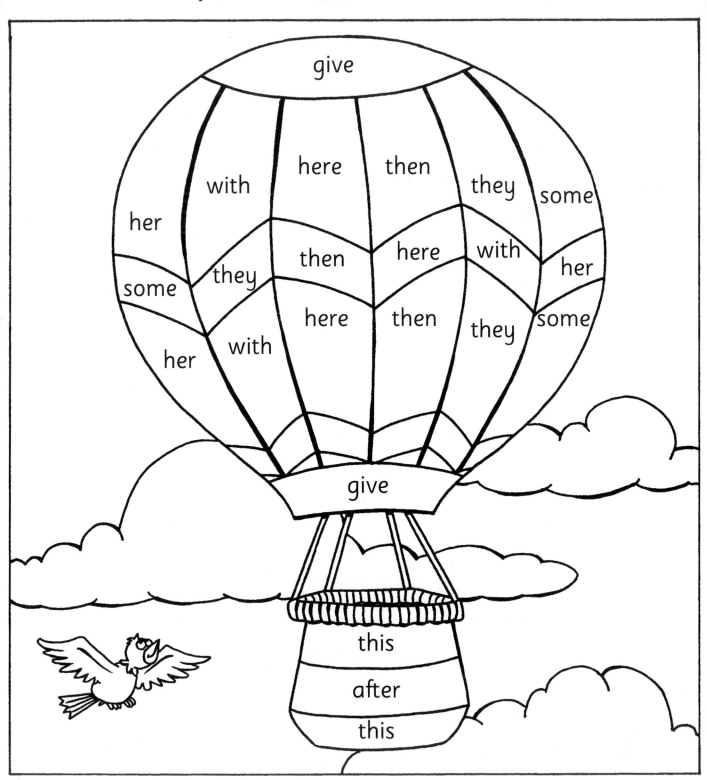

2 **Write the words in the correct cloud.**

there these
when them
other that

4-letter words

5-letter words

3 **Join the matching words.**

| come | their | leave | thing | have | what |

| leave | have | thing | what | come | their |

1 Trace and copy each word.

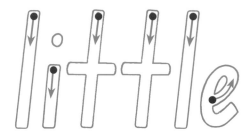 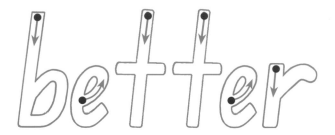

_____   _____

2 Help Issy Me to get to the pretty flowers. Colour the path of pretty words.

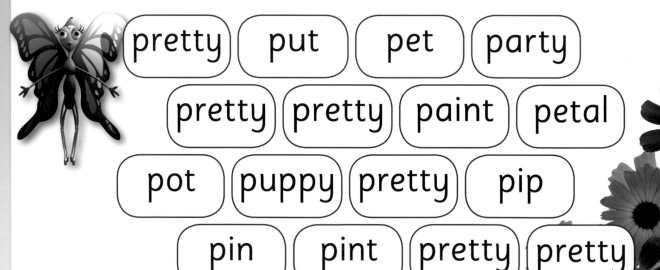

| pretty | put | pet | party |

| pretty | pretty | paint | petal |

| pot | puppy | pretty | pip |

| pin | pint | pretty | pretty |

3 Complete the words.

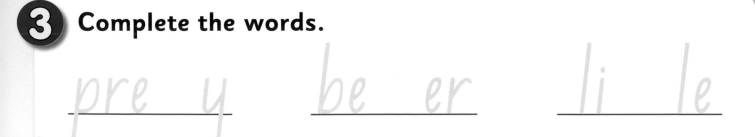

pre___y   be___er   li___le

_____   _____   _____

4 **Draw.**

A pretty bunch of flowers for
Dotty Sun Spot.

A little bone for
Gutter Mutt.

5 **Circle the words.**

little   better   pretty

Poor Wheely Whale. He was feeling
a little bit sick. Zen Ten drew him a
pretty picture. That made Wheely
Whale feel much better.

**Colour a picture each
time you find a word.** ☐ ☐ ☐

CHALLENGE
Find a word in your list that means the same as:
small   lovely   not sick

63

1 Join the word to a picture that rhymes.

which

who

while

2 Complete. **Who are you?**

Sunny Snail

Octo Puss

Xpanda

Who has eight legs? _____

Who is black and white? _____

Who has a shell? _____

3 Complete the words.

_wh_ _____   _____ _ich_   _____ _o_

4 Crack the code!

w = ✿
h = ▲
i = ✓
l = ★
e = ●
o = ■
c = ✹
n = ✚

1 ✿ ▲ ■ _____

2 ✿ ▲ ✓ ✹ ▲ _____

3 ✿ ▲ ✓ ★ ● _____

4 ▲ ■ ✿ _____

5 ✿ ▲ ● ✚ _____

6 ✚ ■ ✿ _____

5 Circle the correct word. Cross out the wrong word.

Wait a while which before you go swimming, Frogfish.

While Who does this hat belong to?

Which While pencil is mine?

CHALLENGE
Write sentences using these words.
who   which   while

1 Join the pieces. Write the words.

_____

_____

_____

2 Colour **could** = pink, **colour** **would** = blue, **colour** **should** = green.

| could | would | should | could |
| should | would | could | should |

3 Complete the words.

coul _____   shou _____   w _____ d

4

Draw a picture of yourself here.

Answer yes or no.

Could you eat 10 ice creams? yes no

Should you brush your teeth? yes no

Would you like to fly to the moon? yes no

5 **Complete the sentences.** could Would should

_____ you like to play with Buzzle Top?

You _____ tell a grown up before you go out.

I _____ run faster than Dan.

CHALLENGE
Write these words in alphabetical order.
would could should

1 Complete. said

"I can tell the time," _____ Tick Tock Clock.

"I have a lot of spines," _____ Hedgehog Dog.

"Zoom, zoom! I can go very fast," _____ Eggster.

2 Find the matching pairs.

pair

again

again

pair

again

pair

pair

again

3 Help Socky Fox to find his pair of socks. Draw a track of said again pair words.

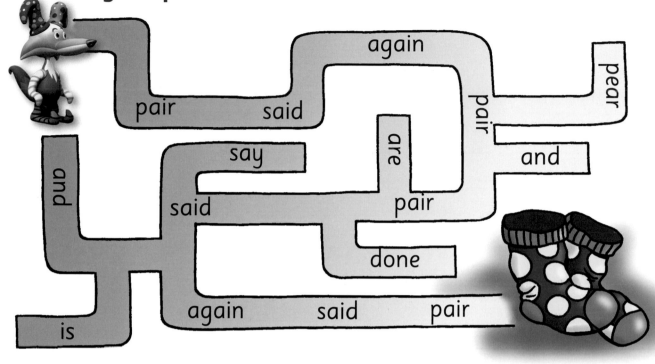

again · pair · said · pear · pair · and · say · are · said · and · pair · done · is · again · said · pair

4 Circle the words.

said again pair

"Hello!" said Yabby Dabby Do. "I have a pair of big claws. SNAP! SNAP!" Yabby, can you snap your claws again?

Colour a picture each time you find a word.

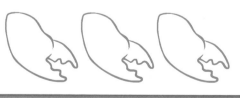

CHALLENGE Circle the hidden words.

esaidfgagainvwpairdnagain

1 Join Wrecking Ball to the word house.

house   has

mouse   house

hose   his

house

2 Trace and copy each word.

_____   _____

3 Colour the word out.

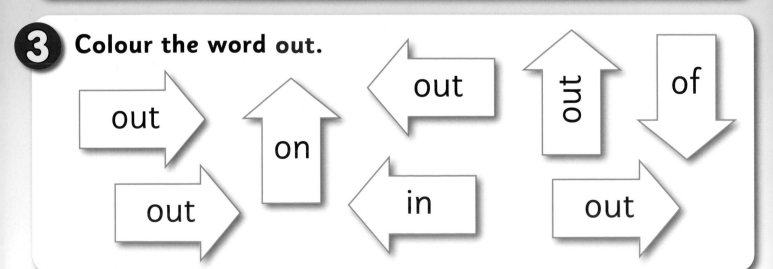

out

out   on   out   of

in   out

4 **Complete.**

Colour the book about dogs = blue.
Colour the book about fish = orange.
Colour the book about cats = green.
Colour the book about birds = red.

5 **Circle the correct word. Cross out the wrong word.**

Alphapet read a story out about rabbits.

Can we play at your house out today?

Let's go house out to the park.

CHALLENGE
Write 3 sentences about your house.

Lesson 30 • all, shall, will

1
Colour all = yellow, colour shall = pink, colour will = blue.

2
Guess the word by its shape. Write each word in a box.

all   shall   will

3
Circle the matching words in each row.

all	and	all	are
shall	she	shell	shall
will	we	will	wall

4 Help Red Rabbit to find all his carrots. Colour the path of **all** words.

all	all	bell	ball	fall
fall	all	ill	hill	tell
call	all	wall	sell	full
mill	all	all	all	all

5 Complete the sentences.

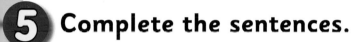

all   will   Shall

Have you eaten _____ of the cake, Catty Cake?

_____ I close the window?

Big Pig, _____ you play with me?

CHALLENGE
Write these words in alphabetical order.

will   all   shall

Choose one word to write in a sentence.

73

1 **Trace and copy each word.**

_____   _____

2 **Guess the word by its shape. Write each word in a box.**

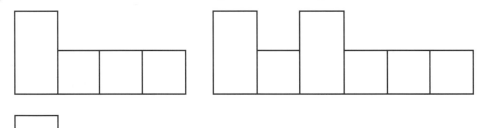

because

before

been

3 **Colour the answers.**

What comes before ?

What comes before ?

What comes before  ?

What comes before  ?

4 **Complete.** Because

Wobble Blob was not very hungry

_____ he ate 5 ice creams.

_____ he ate too much jelly.

_____ he ate a box of popcorn.

5 **Circle the words.**

because   before   been

Where have you been, Gemma? We must go and visit Peggy Leg before it gets too late. Bring your hat because it is very sunny.

Colour a hat each time you find a word.

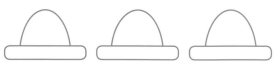

CHALLENGE
Write 4 reasons for not wanting to go to bed.
Start each sentence with: I don't want to
go to bed **because...**

1 **Colour also = blue, colour always = yellow, colour along = green.**

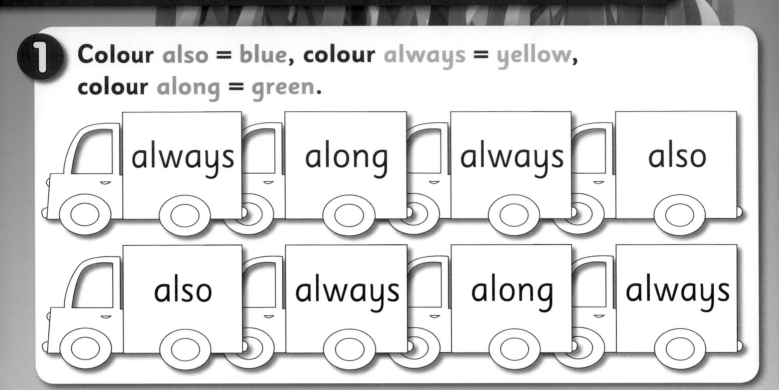

always along always also

also always along always

2 **Complete the sentences.** also

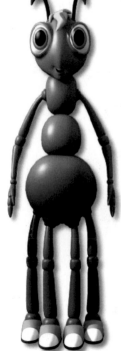

Sam the Ant went to the shops. He bought shoes.

He _____ bought a hat.

He _____ bought a coat.

He _____ bought a bag.

He _____ bought a scarf.

3 **Make words with these letters.**

s l w a y a

1-letter word: ◯

3-letter word: ◯ ◯ ◯

4-letter word: ◯ ◯ ◯ ◯

6-letter word: ◯ ◯ ◯ ◯ ◯ ◯ ◯

4 **Complete the sentences.**

also   always   along

Smile loves pies. He _____
likes to wear ties.

Tug Boat Bug sails _____ the river.

You are _____ sleepy, Happy Nap.

Airy Fairy can fly. She can _____ skip and jump.

CHALLENGE
How many words can you make from the letters
along. (You can only use each letter once.)
3 — good! 4 — great! + 5 — WOW!

1 Join each word to a picture that rhymes.

pair

who

said

house

while

been

all

2 Write the words in the correct box.

pretty	better
shall	should
again	about

5-letter words

6-letter words

③ **Find the words. Colour:** along = red   would = blue
                                   again = pink   about = orange
                                   house = green   which = yellow

w	h	i	c	h	a	b	o	u	t
a	l	o	n	g	a	g	a	i	n
h	o	u	s	e	w	o	u	l	d
w	h	i	c	h	h	o	u	s	e
a	g	a	i	n	w	o	u	l	d
a	l	o	n	g	a	b	o	u	t
w	h	i	c	h	h	o	u	s	e
w	o	u	l	d	a	l	o	n	g
h	o	u	s	e	a	g	a	i	n
a	b	o	u	t	w	o	u	l	d
a	g	a	i	n	w	h	i	c	h
a	l	o	n	g	h	o	u	s	e